The Greatest Battles in His

By Charles

A modern illustration depicting an Ancient Greek phalanx formation

About Charles River Editors

Charles River Editors provides superior editing and original writing services across the digital publishing industry, with the expertise to create digital content for publishers across a vast range of subject matter. In addition to providing original digital content for third party publishers, we also republish civilization's greatest literary works, bringing them to new generations of readers via ebooks.

Sign up here to receive updates about free books as we publish them, and visit Our Kindle Author Page to browse today's free promotions and our most recently published Kindle titles.

Introduction

Adam Carr's picture of the site of the battle today

The Battle of Marathon (490 BCEE)

"The Athenians...charged the barbarians at a run. Now the distance between the two armies was little short of eight furlongs [about a mile]. The Persians, therefore, when they saw the Greeks coming on at speed, made ready to receive them, although it seemed to them that the Athenians were bereft of their senses, and bent upon their own destruction; for they saw a mere handful of men coming on at a run without either horsemen or archers. Such was the opinion of the barbarians; but the Athenians in close array fell upon them, and fought in a manner worthy of being recorded. They were the first of the Greeks, so far as I know, who introduced the custom of charging the enemy at a run, and they were likewise the first who dared to look upon the Persian garb, and to face men clad in that fashion. Until this time the very name of the Persians had been a terror to the Greeks to hear." - Herodotus

The names of history's most famous battles still ring in our ears today, their influence immediately understood by all. Marathon lent its name to the world's most famous race, but it also preserved Western civilization during the First Persian War. Saratoga, won by one of the colonists' most renowned war heroes before he became his nation's most vile traitor. Hastings ensured the Normans' success in England and changed the course of British history. Waterloo, which marked the reshaping of the European continent and Napoleon's doom, has now become part of the English lexicon. In Charles River Editors' Greatest Battles in History series, readers can get caught up to speed on history's greatest battles in the time it takes to finish a commute, while learning interesting facts long forgotten or never known.

The Ancient Greeks have long been considered the forefathers of modern Western civilization, but the Golden Age of Athens and the spread of Greek influence across much of the known world only occurred due to one of the most crucial battles of antiquity: the Battle of Marathon. In 491 B.C., following a successful invasion of Thrace over the Hellespont, the Persian emperor Darius sent envoys to the main Greek city-states, including Sparta and Athens, demanding tokens of earth and water as symbols of submission, but Darius didn't exactly get the reply he sought. According to Herodotus in his famous *Histories*, "Xerxes however had not sent to Athens or to Sparta heralds to demand the gift of earth, and for this reason, namely because at the former time when Dareios had sent for this very purpose, the one people threw the men who made the demand into the pit and the others into a well, and bade them take from thence earth and water and bear them to the king."

Thus, in 490 B.C., after the revolt in Ionia had been crushed, Darius sent his general Mardonius, at the head of a massive fleet and invading force, to destroy the meddlesome Greeks, starting with Athens. The Persian army, numbering anywhere between 30,000 and 300,000 men, landed on the plain at Marathon, a few dozen miles from Athens, where an Athenian army of 10,000 hoplite heavy infantry supported by 1,000 Plataeans prepared to contest their passage. The Athenians appealed to the Spartans for help, but the Spartans dithered; according to the Laws of Lycurgus, they were forbidden to march until the waxing moon was full. Accordingly, their army arrived too late. Thus, it fell upon the Athenians to shoulder the burden. With their army led by the great generals Miltiades and Themistocles, the Athenians charged the outnumbering Persians. Outmatched by the might of the heavy, bronze-armored Greek phalanx, the inferior Persian infantry was enveloped and destroyed, causing them to flee for their ships in panic. The Athenians had won a colossal victory against an overwhelming and seemingly invincible enemy.

Somewhat ironically, the Battle of Marathon has been best commemorated by the race that bears its name, a tradition that started based on a legend that a Greek man named Pheidippides ran the 26.2 miles back to Athens in order to announce the Greek victory and subsequently collapsed and died as soon as he had done so. However, the importance of the battle itself cannot be overstated. The Battle of Marathon proved to be one of the biggest sources of enmity between the Greeks and Persians, and Darius's son Xerxes would seek to undo the results with his own invasion just years later. As it was, the rivalry between the Greeks and Persians would last for over 150 years and culminated with Alexander the Great's destruction of the Achaemenid Persian capital city of Persepolis. Marathon also positioned the city-state of Athens as a major power not only in Greece but throughout the Mediterranean and Near East, as their military, diplomatic, and economic influence grew after the battle.

The Greatest Battles in History: The Battle of Marathon chronicles the decisive Greek victory that ended the First Persian War and ensured the safety of mainland Greece. Along with pictures and a bibliography, you will learn about the Battle of Marathon like never before, in no time at all.

The Greatest Battles in History: The Battle of Marathon
About Charles River Editors
Introduction
   Primary Sources
   Chapter 1: The Ionian Revolt
   Chapter 2: The Achaemenid Persian Perspective of Athens and Ionia
   Chapter 3: The Persians Prepare to Invade Greece
   Chapter 4: The Order of Battle
   Chapter 5: The Athenians Take the Field
   Chapter 6: The Greek Center Collapses
   Chapter 7: The Persian Retreat
   Chapter 8: A Shield Signal?
   Chapter 9: How the Greeks Won the Battle of Marathon
   Chapter 10: The Marathon Runner
   Chapter 11: The Results and Aftermath of the Battle of Marathon
   Bibliography

Primary Sources

As with any historical study, historians' examination of the Battle of Marathon is based on primary sources, and the most complete source concerning the Battle of Marathon is the ancient Greek historian Herodotus' *The Histories*. Herodotus' account has continued to be the base for most modern accounts of the battle, but it's important to recognize inherent flaws in the author's work. While Herodotus is remembered as the "Father of History" for being the first of his kind to write the kind of historical narratives people are familiar with today, he wrote his seminal work decades after the battle and never witnessed the event personally. As a result, his account is based on a number of different oral testimonies, which can be full of inherent problems (Vansina 1985, 3-32).

An ancient bust depicting Herodotus

Herodotus' account is also relatively short and lacks some important details. For example, the time of year or week of the battle is never given, and he doesn't specify how many days the whole episode lasted, from the preparations on the field to the time when the Persians sailed back to Asia. To corroborate Herodotus, modern scholars also have the 1st century CE Greek geographer Pausanias and his work *Description of Greece*. Pausanias is perhaps best used as an auxiliary to Herodotus, as he wrote much later and his descriptions of Marathon were more concerned with burial sites of the fallen warriors then the battle itself.

The final sources for the reconstruction of the Battle of Marathon then are modern archaeologists and historians. Modern scholars have helped to fill in considerable gaps in knowledge concerning the Battle of Marathon by conducting digs that have verified different aspects of the Herodotus account and by using philology to better understand the detailed nuances of what the ancient Greek historian wrote.

By combining all of these sources, not only can a reasonable reconstruction of the Battle of Marathon be made, but perhaps some new ideas may come to light.

Chapter 1: The Ionian Revolt

A 5th century depiction of a Greek hoplite (right) fighting a Persian soldier

The Battle of Marathon was part of the wider Greco-Persian Wars (499-479 BCE), which began on the Ionian coastline (modern day western Turkey) but would later spread to directly affect mainland Greek city-states such as Athens and Sparta. In 500 BCE, Sparta and Athens were not terribly interested in the affairs of the Achaemenid Persian Empire, and for the most part, the status of the Ionian Greeks, who were under Persian control, also mattered very little to them. Sparta stood at the head of an alliance/league of Peloponnesian city-states who were more concerned with their region, while Athens had recently abolished tyranny and was learning the intricacies of democratic government (Forrest 2001, 37).

While Athens was uninvolved, perhaps following the cue of their Athenian cousins, some of the Ionian, Aeolian, and Doric city-states in Anatolia revolted against their own tyrants, which was tantamount to rebellion against their Persian overlords (Forrest 2001, 37). Herodotus provided the best account of the Ionian Revolt, which was largely instigated by a former tyrant named Aristagoras, who believed that a successful revolt would place him in a powerful position. Herodotus wrote, "Certain substantial citizens of Naxos, forced by the commons to leave the island, took refuge in Miletus, which had been put under Aristagoras, son of Molpagoras, as deputy governor. He was nephew and son-in-law of Histiaeus, the son of Lysagoras, who was being detained by Darius at Susa . . . The first thing they did when they got there was to ask Aristagoras to lend them some troops, in the hope of recovering their position at home. This suggested to Aristagoras that if he helped the exiles to return he himself would be ruler of Naxos; so using their friendship with Histiaeus to cloak his purpose, he made them an offer." (Herodotus, *The Histories*, V, 30).

Aristagoras had a keen sense of political acumen and a feel for the times, as a large part of his strategy was to gain the favor of the Ionians Greeks by promising the reward of democracy. First, he had to abdicate his own tyranny, which he did in public fashion. According to Herodotus, "To induce the Milesians to support him, he began by professing to abdicate his tyranny in favor of a popular government, and then went on to do the same thing in the other Ionian states, where he got rid of the tyrants." (Herodotus, *The Histories*, V, 37).

At the same time, Aristagoras knew that enticing the Ionian states to rebel would not be enough to defeat the mighty Achaemenid Empire. For that, he would need the support of one, or both, of the Ionian's mainland Greek cousins. However, Aristagoras' efforts to obtain the aid of Sparta and Athens against the Persians would lead to his demise and set the Athenians on a crash course with the Persians that would reach its apex at Marathon.

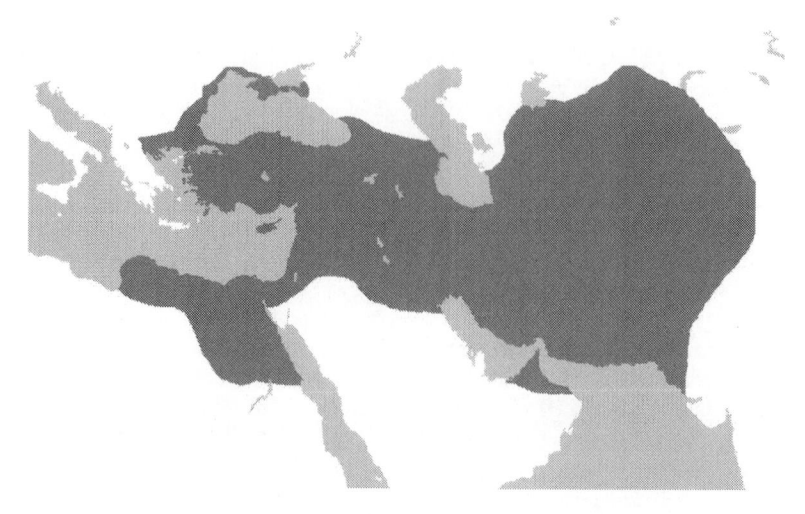

A map depicting the enormous extent of the Achaemenid Empire

Perhaps owing to the fierce reputation of the Spartan warriors, or simply due to the fact that Sparta was farthest from Ionia, Aristagoras visited Sparta first to plead for assistance against the Persians. At the time, Sparta's government was a type of republican-monarchy, in which adult males had voting rights at their councils but two kings presided over the city and largely decided on affairs of state such as diplomacy and war (Plutarch, *Lycurgus*, 7). When Aristagoras finally made it to Sparta, he met with the only reigning king of the time, Cleomenes, and at first tried to appeal to his patriotism, then his pride, and finally his greed. Herodotus' account of Aristagoras' plea to Cleomenes reads, "I hope Cleomenes, that you will not be too much surprised at my anxiety to visit you. The circumstances are these. That Ionians should have become slaves in place of free men is a bitter shame and grief not only to us, but to the rest of Greece, and especially to you, who are the leaders of the Greek world. We beg you, therefore, in the name of the gods of Greece, to save from slavery your Ionian kinsmen. It will be an easy task, for these foreigners have little taste for war, and you are the finest soldiers in the world. The Persian weapons are bows and short spears; they fight in trousers and turbans – that will show you how easy they are to beat! Moreover, the inhabitants of that continent are richer than all the rest of the world put together – they have everything, gold, silver, bronze, elaborately embroidered clothes and beasts of burden and slaves. All this you may have if you wish." (Herodotus, *The Histories*, V, 49).

Cleomenes' interest was apparently piqued until Aristagoras showed him a map of the vast Achaemenid Empire, to which the Spartan replied, "Your proposal to take Lacedaemonians a three months' journey from the sea is a highly improper one." (Herodotus, *The Histories*, V, 50).

Unfazed by the Spartans' denial of his proposal, Aristagoras began to sail back to Ionia, but he stopped in Athens to present the citizens of that city-state with a similar offer. Aristagoras approached the Athenians at an opportune time, as they had recently expelled their tyrant Hippias, who was supported by the Persians, so they were already inclined to campaign against them (Herodotus, *The Histories*, V, 97). Aristagoras used many of the same arguments he tried with the Spartans, including the weakness of the Persian military and the riches of the Achaemenid Empire, but he also appealed to common ancestry that the Athenians and Ionians shared. Herodotus noted, "In addition to this he pointed out that Miletus had been founded by Athenian settlers, so it was only natural that the Athenians, powerful as they were, should help her in her need. Once persuaded to accede to Aristagoras' appeal, the Athenians passed a decree for the dispatch of twenty ships to Ionia, under the command of Melanthius, a distinguished Athenian." (Herodotus, *The Histories*, V, 97).

Athenian support for the Ionian cause was lukewarm at best, and the entire Ionian coalition soon crumbled under the weight of the mighty Achaemenid Empire. When the Persians were finally able to reestablish their rule over the rebellious Ionian city-states, Aristagoras fled and later died in exile, and the rebellious cities, especially Miletus, suffered under brutal punitive measures. (Herodotus, *The Histories*, V, 126). Herodotus graphically wrote about the punishment the Persians meted out to the Ionians: "Once the towns were in their hands, the best-looking boys were chosen for castration and made into eunuchs; the most beautiful girls were dragged from their homes and sent to Darius' court, and the towns themselves, temples and all, were burnt to the ground." (Herodotus, *The Histories*, VI, 32).

The ruthless suppression of the Ionian Revolt by the Achaemenid Persians proved to be the first act in the greater Greco-Persian Wars, and if the Athenians thought that their limited involvement in the affair would mitigate the ire of the Persian king Darius I (ca. 550-486 BCE), they were sorely mistaken. Through their involvement in the Ionian Revolt, despite the fact it was minimal for the most part, the Athenians set themselves at odds with the Persian emperor, putting them on a crash course that would culminate at the Battle of Marathon about nine years later.

An ancient depiction of Darius I

Chapter 2: The Achaemenid Persian Perspective of Athens and Ionia

When the Battle of Marathon took place in 490 BCE, Athens was a powerful city-state, but it was just one among many that were as prone to fight each other as they were non-Greeks. The Persians on the other hand commanded the greatest empire the known world had ever witnessed – the Achaemenid Empire – which spanned from Bactria (present day Afghanistan) in the east to Egypt in the west (Briant 2002, 366). Besides possessing the already ancient and venerated kingdom of Egypt, the Achaemenid Persians also controlled the city of Babylon and the regions of Mesopotamia and the Levant, which were home to such illustrious previous cultures as Israel, the Phoenicians, and the Assyrians just to name a few. When viewed from this perspective, the Greek Ionian city-states were a small fraction of the total empire, and the more distant Athenians may have appeared to the Persians as little more than minor interlopers who were playing a dangerous game that was out of their league. That said, despite the fact that the Persians in general may have disregarded any military threat that the Athenians posed, Ionia was still viewed as an important part of the Achaemenid Empire.

The Achaemenid Empire was divided in satrapies, or provinces, which were generally based more on ethnicity than geographical area, although the two often coincided (Cameron 1973). The number of satrapies also fluctuated, although there were usually at least 20 at any time (Briant 2002, 390). A number of extant Persian satrapal lists are known from the reign of Darius I, which includes ones from the royal palace at Persepolis, Darius' royal tomb, and a colossal statue of the ruler discovered in the ruins of Susa in 1972 (Roaf 1974, 149). Herodotus also gives a list of 20 satrapies and the type and amount of tribute they brought to Persepolis in Book III of *The Histories*. Ionia was listed in some of these lists as a satrapy, and Herodotus' account in particular noted that the Ionia was responsible for a yearly tribute payment of 400 talents of silver (Herodotus, *The Histories*, III, 90). The satrapy of Ionia was clearly an important possession to the Achaemenid Persians, which in their eyes justified the level of brutality they used in order to bring the province back into line.

The Athenians no doubt raised the ire of Darius I when they supported the Ionian Revolt, but their direct interference in the affairs of the Achaemenid Empire was not their first transgression against the Persians. Before the Athenians inserted themselves into the Ionian Revolt, they were involved in a war with Sparta, and when that did not go well for them, they looked to Persia for an alliance. The Athenians sent envoys to the city of Sardis in Ionia to meet with the Persian governor, Artaphernes, who requested that the Greeks give a symbolic gift of earth and water to him. Herodotus explained, "To strengthen their position they sent representatives to Sardis, in the hope of concluding an alliance with Persia. When they got there and delivered their message, Artaphernes the son of Hystaspes, the governor, asked in reply who these Athenians were that sought an alliance with Persia, and in what part of the world they lived. Then, having been told, he put the Persian case in a nutshell by remarking that, if the Athenians would signify their submission by the usual gift of earth and water, then Darius would make a pact with them; otherwise they had better go home. Eager that the pact should be concluded, the envoys acted on their own initiative and accepted Artaphernes' terms – for which they were severely censured on their return to Athens." (Herodotus, *The Histories*, V, 73).

As Herodotus wrote, the Athenian envoys were admonished for their act of obeisance towards the Persians, but the political damage had been done; the Athenians broke Persian protocol and tradition when they offered earth and water but did not give their obedience. Furthermore, around the time of the Athenian earth and water fiasco, Hippias, the tyrant who was expelled from Athens in 510 BCE, showed up in Sardis and urged Artaphernes and the Persians to restore him as tyrant of Athens (Olmstead 1948, 151-52). In fact, when the Persians finally set forward with their invasion plan of Greece, Hippias was with the Persian fleet, which indicates that the invasion was at least partially intended to restore Athens to tyranny (Doenges 1998, 2).

By breaking the standard Persian political protocol, the Athenians had placed themselves on the imperial radar of the Persians, but when they supported the Ionian Revolt, Darius I took the matter personally. The Persians were not the only one who committed atrocities during the

Ionian Revolt, as a combined force of Ionian Greeks and Athenians captured and sacked the city of Sardis and reduced its temple to rubble. When Darius I learned of the Athenians role in the sack of Sardis, he exploded. According to Herodotus, "The story goes that when Darius learnt of the disaster, he did not give a thought to the Ionians, knowing perfectly well that the punishment for their revolt would come; but he asked who the Athenians were, and then, on being told, called for his bow. He took it, set an arrow on the string, shot it up into the air and cried: 'Grant, O God, that I may punish the Athenians.'" (Herodotus, *The Histories*, V, 105).

To Darius I, the matter was settled: the Athenians must be taught a lesson and brought under the yoke of the Achaemenid Empire.

Chapter 3: The Persians Prepare to Invade Greece

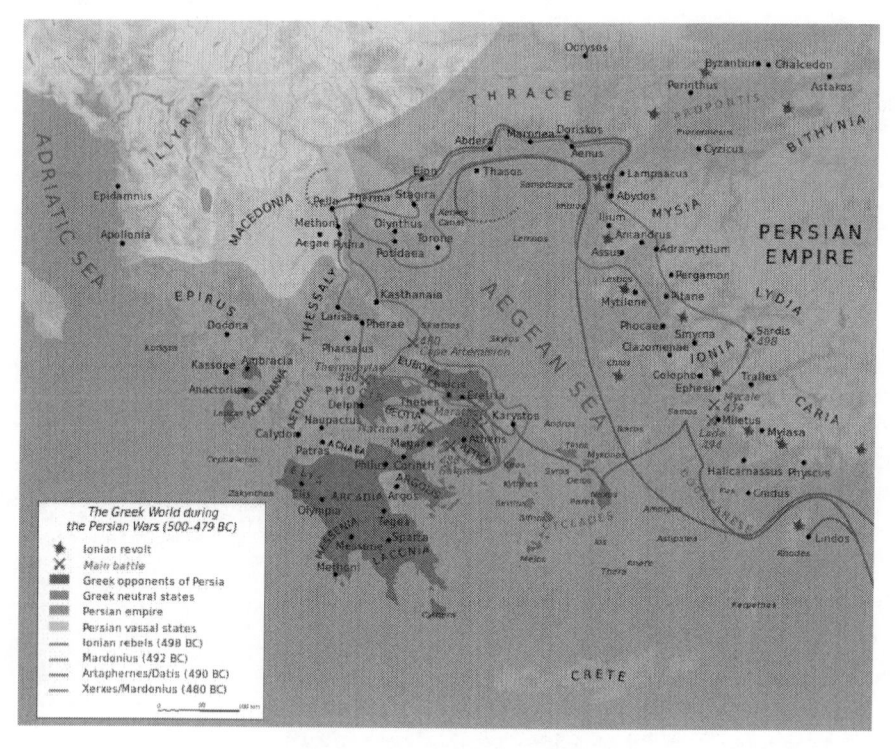

A map of the region from 500-479 BCE

In the ancient world, it took a lot of time and resources to plan a large-scale military campaign, and the Persian invasion of Greece was no exception. The heart of the Achaemenid Empire was thousands of miles from Greece, so any major invasion would involve many logistical concerns, especially transportation of troops and resources, but Darius I was up for the challenge. The Persian army was led by the general Mardonius, who mustered his forces on land and sea in Ionia in 491 BCE, and his expedition into Greece would be the largest military expedition that world had ever seen. In fact, it was most likely intended to subjugate not only Athens but all of Greece.

From Ionia, Mardonius led the Persian army north along the Aegean coastline until they marched through Thrace and Macedonia. At this point, they encountered a storm that destroyed most of their ships (Herodotus, *The Histories*, VI, 44). The disastrous loss of the Persian fleet only proved to be a temporary setback though, as the rich Achaemenid Empire was able to muster a new army, which was led by a general named Datis. Datis was ordered by Darius I to "reduce Athens and Eretria to slavery and to bring the slaves before the king." (Herodotus, *The Histories*, VI, 94).

Datis had many advantages over the Greeks, as he commanded overwhelming naval superiority and had the military intelligence of Hippias, the former tyrant of Athens, at his disposal (Doenges 1998, 2). Instead of following Mardonius' route the previous year around the Aegean, Datis led the Persian army by ships directly across the Aegean, reducing the island of Naxos to slavery but sparing Delos (Herodotus, *The Histories*, VI, 95-98).

When Datis and the Persians arrived in Greece, they first set their sights on laying waste to Eretria. According to Herodotus, the Eretrians prepared themselves for a long siege but were betrayed by some of their own people: "The Eretrians had no intention of leaving their defenses to meet the coming attack in the open; their one concern (the proposal not to abandon the town having been carried) was to defend their walls – if they could . . . then on the seventh, two well-known Eretrians, Euphorbus the son of Alcimachus and Philagrus the son of Cyneas, betrayed the town to the enemy. The Persians entered, and stripped the temples bare and burnt them in revenge for the burnt temples of Sardis, and, in accordance with Darius' orders, carried off all the inhabitants as slaves." (Herodotus, *The* Histories, VI, 101)

With Eretria reduced to rubble, Datis then turned his attention south to the Attica peninsula and the city of Athens, but unlike the Eretrians, the Athenians would be better prepared and would leave their city to meet the Persians on the plain near Marathon.

Chapter 4: The Order of Battle

A picture of reconstructed Persian ships on the beach near the Battle of Marathon

Before the Battle of Marathon, the Athenians had plenty of time to plan and mobilize for war, and after the Persians defeated the Ionians and then obliterated Eretria, the Athenians were able to put a plan into action that is still admired and studied by military historians. Although Athens was a decent sized city-state for the Hellenic world, it was puny compared to the Achaemenid Empire, making it impossible to make up for the numerical disparity in a number of ways.

Nonetheless, Athens was still formidable. All Athenian citizens between the ages of 18-42 were eligible for military service (Sage 1996, 38), and the army was sub-divided by tribes, which were then commanded by lieutenants known as *taxiarchs* (Sage 1996, 38). Although the requirements for and basic structure of the Athenian military are known, much less is known about the men's training. During the period of the Battle of Marathon, there is no evidence for any formal training of hoplites in Athens, and the only Greek city-state where any significant training is recorded comes from Sparta (Sage 1996, 35). In other words, the Athenian military at the time of the Battle of Marathon was a sort of "home guard," where each male citizen was responsible for his part militarily and thus always prepared for war.

As noted before, Herodotus is the most complete primary source concerning the Battle of Marathon, but others do exist or at least once did, that can help complement Herodotus' account. The oldest sources that depicted the Battle of Marathon were actually a series of pictures that were painted in the Poecile Stoa by the artists Micon and Paenus around 460 BCE, about 30 years after the battle (Hammond 1968, 26). Unfortunately, the pictures are no longer extant, but the Greek geographer Pausanias gave a partial description in his geographic survey of Greece: "At the end of the painting are those who fought at Marathon; the Boeotians of Plataea and the Attic contingent are coming to blows with the foreigners. In this place neither side has the better, but the centre of the fighting shows the foreigners in flight and pushing one another into the morass, while at the end of the painting are the Phoenician ships, and the Greeks killing the foreigners who are scrambling into them." (Pausanias, *Description of Greece*, I, 5.3). Pausanias' description of the Poecile Stoa is useful because it corroborates Herodotus' accounts, namely that the Plataeans were the only other Greeks besides the Athenians who fought the Persians. It also indicates the chaos of the Persians' retreat.

The battle of Marathon itself is believed to have taken place in September 490 BCE (Hammond 1968), and it is also thought to be the first amphibious battle in world history (Doenges 1998, 4). The Persians landed their invasion force near Marathon because it was believed to be good ground for them to maneuver their cavalry, which the Persian commander Datis believed would give him the edge over the Greek hoplites (Hammond 1968, 33). Although the plain around Marathon was good ground for cavalry and was no doubt a large part of the Persian decision to land there, its proximity to Eretria also played a role. Herodotus wrote, "The part of Attic territory nearest Eretria – and also the best ground for cavalry to maneuver in – was at Marathon. To Marathon, therefore, Hippias the son of Pisistratus directed the invading army, and the Athenians, as soon as the news arrived, hurried to meet it. The Athenian troops were commanded by ten generals, of whom the tenth was Miltiades." (Herodotus, *The Histories*, VI, 102-103).

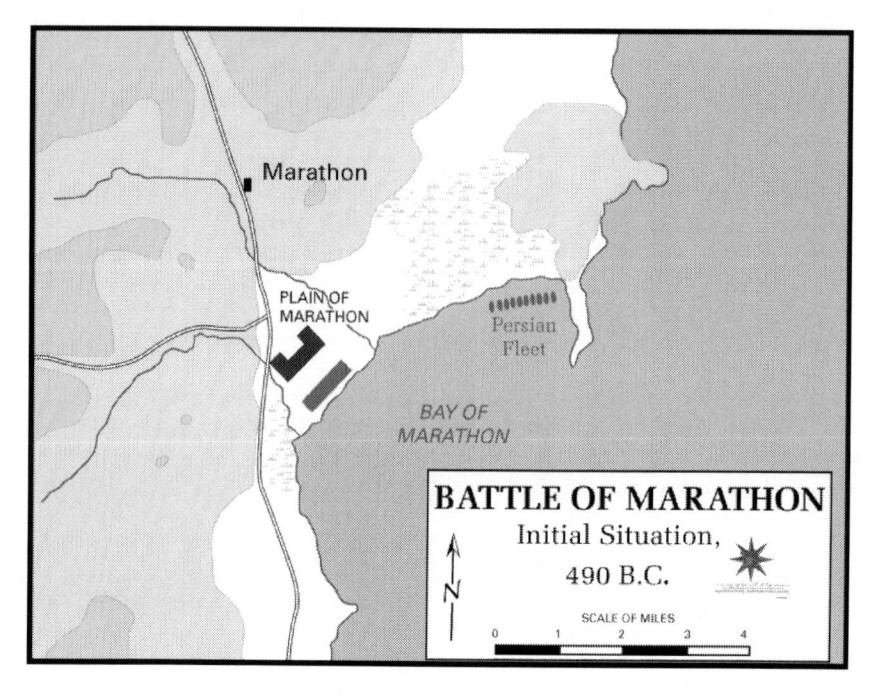

Disposition of the forces at Marathon

The appearance of the former Athenian tyrant, Hippias, is also important because he apparently provided useful intelligence to Datis and the Persians that revealed Marathon to be the best place for cavalry operations. It was also close to the recently conquered Eretria, and the close proximity to Eretria was logistically important to the Persians and their potential success not only at Marathon but also if they were to subject all of Attica and possibly Greece itself. Since the Persian army was so far removed from the nearest Achaemenid colonies (which were across the Aegean in Ionia), they were forced to use Eretria as a temporary base and source of their supply lines (Hammond 1968, 32). The short distance between Eretria and Marathon across the bay also provided a safe and quick route for the Persians to move goods and men.

As a result, the Persians assembled their army near Marathon, but the exact size of the army is still open to conjecture. Unfortunately, Herodotus never gave a number for the combatants in the Persian army – only ships – so modern historians are forced to make educated guesses based on the size of the field, the number that Herodotus listed as killed, and the number of Persian ships. A recent study estimates that the number of Persian fighting men may have been around 12,000-15,000 men, which would not be much more than the army the Greeks fielded at Marathon (Doenges 1998, 6), but earlier studies, such as Hammond's, places the total number of the

Persian army as high as 90,000. That said, Hammond noted that many of them would have been sailors and not infantry (Hammond 1968, 33).

Chapter 5: The Athenians Take the Field

"With you it rests, Callimachus, either to bring Athens to slavery, or, by securing her freedom, to be remembered by all future generations. For never since the time that the Athenians became a people were they in so great a danger as now. If they bow their necks beneath the yoke of the Persians, the woes which they will have to suffer...are already determined. If, on the other hand, they fight and overcome, Athens may rise to be the very first city in Greece." – Miltiades to the polemarch [an honored dignitary of Athens] before the battle, according to Herodotus

Since Athens was a democracy, major decisions of state were decided by a majority vote of either an assembly of the citizens, or as often in the case of war, a vote of the 10 generals mentioned above. The first major decision that the Athenians would face was to either prepare the city's defenses for a siege or wait for help from other Greeks, such as the Spartans, to arrive. The other choice was to meet the much larger Persian force on the battlefield near Marathon. There was merit to both arguments, and in true Greek fashion both sides were heard, but ultimately it was the general Miltiades who swayed the opinion of the other generals to meet the Persians on the battlefield: "Amongst the Athenian commanders opinion was divided: some were against risking a battle, on the ground that the Athenian force was too small to stand a chance of success; others – and amongst them Miltiades – urged it . . . To Callimachus, therefore, Miltiades turned. 'It is now in your hands, Callimachus,' he said, 'either to enslave Athens, or to make her free and to leave behind you for all future generations a memory more glorious than even Harmodius and Aristogeiton left. Never in our history have we Athenians been in such peril as now. If we submit to the Persians, Hippias will be restored to power – and there is little doubt what misery must then ensue: but if we fight and win, then this city of ours may well grow to pre-eminence amongst all the cities of Greece' . . . Miltiades' words prevailed, and by the vote of Callimachus the War Archon the decision to fight was made." (Herodotus, *The Histories*, VI, 109-110).

The Athenians thus decided to meet the Persians on the battlefield, and it is generally believed that they took the northern route from Athens to Marathon, which is about 25 miles long (Doegnes 1998, 7). The only other road to Marathon was slightly longer at about 28 miles and would have left the Greeks more exposed to a cavalry attack (Doegnes 1998, 7). After the Greeks arrived, the two sides faced each other in an uneasy calm that lasted for a few days before the battle, which helped the Greeks fortify their forces and better prepare for battle.

Once the Greeks arrived on the plain, they camped at a site that was considered to be sacred to the hero Hercules, and they were then joined by the Plataean Greek contingent. According to Herodotus, "The Athenian troops were drawn up on a piece of ground sacred to Heracles, when they were joined by the Plataeans, who came to support them with every available man."

(Herodotus, *The Histories*, VI, 108).

The total number of Greeks who were camped at the plain near Marathon is estimated to be around 10,000 total, with about 1,000 of the hoplites being Plataeans (Hammond 1968, 34). Although most of the Athenian hoplites traveled to Marathon to confront the Persians, a small skeleton crew stayed behind in Athens in order to defend the city in case the Persian forces split and part attacked the city (Hammond 1968, 34).

Datis and the Persians were eager to engage the Greeks in battle as they had the advantage with numbers and cavalry, but the Greeks were not yet done with their preparations that would help give them the ultimate advantage. In the days before the actual battle, the Greeks probably gradually advanced their position, felling trees along the way and then using those trees to obstruct the Persian cavalry (Hammond 1968, 39). Thus, by the time the Greeks had advanced to the actual battlefield, they tried to be protected in their rear and flanks by the rugged hillsides, which effectively made the Persian cavalry useless (Hammond 1968, 39). This strategy was a major factor in how the Greeks won the battle, because the vaunted and feared Persian cavalry played almost no role in the Battle of Marathon, and the Greek hoplites were much better armored and trained than the average Persian soldiers, who wore little armor.

Chapter 6: The Greek Center Collapses

In essence, Miltiades and the Greeks knew that in order to defeat the larger Persian army they had to plan accordingly and win the battle before the first blow was struck, while Datis became too reliant on his cavalry and was unwilling to improvise. Still, while the decisions made by Miltiades and Datis before the actual battle may have ultimately decided the victor, the two sides still had to fight, and it turned out to be an epic battle that has rightfully earned its legendary reputation.

In pre-modern warfare, the standard order of battle usually involved the belligerent armies lining up in shield wall, or *phalanx*, across from each other and then fighting with the ultimate goal of breaking through the enemy's line. Herodotus' description of the Battle of Marathon appears to follow this method: "When it did come, the Athenian army moved into position for the coming struggle. The right wing was commanded by Callimachus – for it was the regular practice at that time in Athens that the War Archon should lead the right wing; then followed the tribes, in their regular order; and, finally, on the left wing, were the Plataeans." (Herodotus, *The Histories*, VI, 111).

The fact that the Athenian field marshal (War Archon), Callimachus, was on one of the wings instead of the center is another important aspect of the battle that will be discussed further below, but as the two armies met, the Greeks were forced to compensate for their numerical inferiority, so Callimachus, Miltiades and the other Greek generals were faced with a choice: concentrate their forces in the center (where the initial Persian thrust would probably be focused) or place the majority of their forces on the wings in order to prevent being flanked. According to Herodotus, the Greeks chose the second option: "One result of the disposition of Athenian troops before the battle was the weakening of their center by the effort to extend the line sufficiently to cover the whole Persian front; the two wings were strong, but the line in the centre was only a few ranks deep. The dispositions made, and the preliminary sacrifice promising success, the word was given to move, and the Athenians advanced at a run towards the enemy, not less than a mile away . . . They were the first Greeks, so far as we know, to charge at a run, and the first who dared to look without flinching at Persian dress and the men who wore it; for until that day came, no Greek could hear even the word Persian without terror." (Herodotus, *The Histories*, VI, 112).

Perhaps the most interesting and strategically important aspect of this passage is the fact that the Greeks ran to meet the Persians. At first, one may think that running to meet the enemy on the battlefield would be disadvantageous, especially a mile away, because it could tire the runners out, but there are some advantages to the strategy as well. Combatants in pre-modern battles had to be in good physical shape given the nature of the hand-to-hand fighting, so a brisk run to meet the enemy would raise soldiers' heart rates and help get them in the proper frame of mind as the battle began. In effect, the mile or so that the Greek hoplites ran across the plain of Marathon to meet the Persian army was a warm-up for the main event, which was the actual battle.

Modern scholars have also pointed out that when the Greeks sprinted to meet the Persians, they eliminated one of the advantages that the Persians had: cavalry. Once the two armies became engaged and the Greek flanks were protected by the hilly terrain, the Persian cavalry threat was eliminated (Hammond 1968, 40). The other Persian advantage – numerical superiority – was countered by the Greek formation of the battle line, which would prove to be the ultimate undoing of Datis and his army.

However, once the battle began, it was not long before the thin Greek center collapsed. A burial mound that was discovered and excavated in modern times marks where the Greek center stood, and also where the Greeks suffered most of their casualties (Hammond 1968, 18). Herodotus' account tells how the Persians pushed through the center: "The struggle at Marathon was long and drawn out. In the centre, held by the Persians themselves and the Sacae, the advantage was with the foreigners, who were so far successful as to break the Greek line and pursue the fugitives inland from the sea; but the Athenians on one wing and the Plataeans on the other were both victorious . . . Drawing their two wings together into a single unit, they turned their attention to the Persians who had broken through in the center." (Herodotus, *The Histories*, VI, 113).

The wings were instrumental to Greek victory, as they essentially ceded the center to the Persians but then collapsed on their enemy from the wings. Herodotus, who had no military experience and was not well versed in military affairs, does not mention if the Greeks planned the maneuver in such a way, but logic would seem to indicate that they did. Up until this point in the battle, everything that Miltiades and Callimachus did was precise and well-thought out, from the road they took to Marathon, to where they chose to camp, and even the decision to sprint to engage the Persians. As such, it would be hard to believe that the Greek generals did not plan to collapse the wings as well. Hammond noted, "Now it is obvious that the action of the Athenians and the Plataeans on the wings, which were separated from one another by a considerable distance, had been preconcerted; for Miltiades, having thinned his centre and packed his wings, must have anticipated the actual developments in the fighting and issued orders in advance to the effect that the men on the wings, if and when victorious, were to turn towards the centre, to form line and to go to the aid of the Greek troops of the centre." (Hammond 1968, 29).

Hannibal's victory against the Romans at Cannae has often been considered the seminal use of a pincers attack of this type, and it is still considered a masterpiece of generalship that was imitated about 2,000 years later by Napoleon at Austerlitz, but if Hammond is correct, Miltiades and Callimachus orchestrated a pincers attack at Marathon centuries before Hannibal did. Either way, it's clear that Miltiades and the other Greek generals aided their cause and evened the odds by planning for contingencies. On the other hand, despite numerous advantages, Datis and the Persians were unable to capitalize on their superior numbers at the center of the line, and their cavalry was useless (Doenges 1998, 12).

Chapter 7: The Persian Retreat

"The two armies fought together on the plain of Marathon for a length of time; and in the mid-battle the barbarians were victorious, and broke and pursued the Greeks into the inner country; but on the two wings the Athenians and the Plataeans defeated the enemy . Having so done, they suffered the routed barbarians to fly at their ease, and joining the two wings in one, fell upon those who had broken their own center, and fought and conquered them. These likewise fled, and now the Athenians hung upon the runaways and cut them down, chasing them all the way to the shore, on reaching which they laid hold of the ships and called aloud for fire." - Herodotus

Once the Greek flanks collapsed on the Persian center, Datis knew that phase of the battle was lost, so he ordered the Persians to retreat to the ships. Herodotus wrote very little about the Persian retreat other than that the Greeks captured seven Persians ships and that two Greek generals, Callimachus and Stesilaus, were killed pursuing the Persians (Herodotus, *The Histories*, VI, 114-115), but Pausanias helps fill in the gaps. He wrote that the disastrous Persian retreat may have been partially due to them not knowing the terrain and running into a marsh: "There is at Marathon a lake which for the most part is marshy. Into this ignorance of the roads made the foreigners fall in their flight, and it is said that this accident was the cause of their great losses." (Pausanias, *Geography of Greece*, I, 32,7).

Datis and the Persians were losing, but they were not yet defeated, so he and his surviving army that made it to the ships set sail around the Attic peninsula for Athens (Morkot 1996, 75).

The quickest way for the Persians to reach Athens from Marathon was by land, and preferably on horseback, but once the Greeks defeated them at Marathon, they had to sail the entire way to Athens (Hodge 2001, 247). At this point, the Greek victory on the battlefield of Marathon was assured, but all may have been lost if Datis and the Persians could reach Athens before them. Plutarch succinctly captured the Greek urgency as they raced back to Athens on foot: "When the Athenians had routed the Barbarians and driven them aboard their ships, and saw that they were sailing away, not toward the islands, but into the gulf toward Attica under compulsion of wind and wave, then they were afraid lest the enemy find Athens empty of defenders, and so they hastened homeward with nine tribes, and reached the city that very day. But Aristides was left behind at Marathon with his own tribe, to guard the captives and the booty." (Plutarch, *Aristides*, 4-5).

Chapter 8: A Shield Signal?

As the Greeks raced on foot to protect their precious city, Datis had one last hand to play: traitors within Athens. This may be perhaps the most mysterious aspect of the fighting, as Herodotus' account seems to raise more questions than answers. According to Herodotus, members of the powerful Alcmaeonidae family conspired with Datis and the Persians in some manner. Herodotus wrote, "The Persians laid a course round Sunium for Athens, which they hoped to reach in advance of the Athenian army. In Athens the Alcmaeonidae were accused of suggesting this move; they had, it was said, an understanding with the Persians, and raised a shield as a signal to them when they were already on board. While the Persian fleet was on its way round Sunium, the Athenians hurried back with all possible speed to save their city, and succeeded in reaching it before the arrival of the Persians." (Herodotus, *The Histories*, VI, 116).

Plutarch's later account of the race to Athens by both the Persians and Greeks corroborates Herodotus' account, but the aspect of traitorous elements within Athens is not repeated by later historians, so modern scholars are left to other methods to judge the validity and importance of the account. Herodotus clearly noted that a shield was raised as a signal to the Persian fleet, but he did not specify exactly *how* that shield was used as a signal or what type of message it could have conveyed. It is important to recognize that a hoplite shield could not have given a flash because of its convex shape (Hodge 2001, 237), so this would rule out the shield signal as a heliographic device, and it's unclear whether heliography was even used as a method of communication at the time. But what if what Herodotus described as a shield was really a flat, bronze sheet that was capable of reflection? In theory, this could be done at a range of up to almost three miles, but there are obvious problems with this theory. If the signaler flashed the bronze in a steady transmission for five to ten minutes, then those on the Persian ships would only see split-second flashes, which would mean that they would have to anchor for a period of time in order to decipher the message (Hodge 2001, 245-46). Modern heliographic techniques have primarily used Morse Code as a language, so any ancient heliographic methods would have employed a code yet unknown to modern scholars.

If the Marathon shield signal was not used as a heliographic device, then it was probably raised or waved by the bearer to the fleet that was near the shore (Hodge 2001, 239). This means that the signal was probably pre-arranged, and that the Persians would have known where and when to look for it on the coastline (Hodge 2001, 239). The signal also had to have been simple enough to just relate a two-way choice (Hodge 2001, 239). Perhaps if the bearer waved the shield above his head, it meant one thing, but if he held the shield low, it meant something else.

Whatever the actual movement of the shield was, there can be no doubt that the one wielding it was an Athenian traitor who was probably at the Battle of Marathon (Hodge 2001, 246), and the origin of the traitorous shield bearer can be determined by assessing the context of the situation. Both armies were in a race south for Athens, with the Greeks by land and the Persians by sea, so anyone signaling the Persian fleet had to have been at Marathon and know that both armies were headed south. The Greeks who stayed behind in Athens did not yet know the outcome of the battle, or that the two armies were headed their way.

As such, if there was a shield signal, it was a message to Datis and the Persians that relayed the movements and intents of the Greek army (Hodge 2001, 246). It will probably never be known what message the signal sent, but Hodge thinks that it meant "Abort Loutsa! Plan B, go round Sounion" (Hodge 2001, 253). Hodge points out that a landing at Loutsa would have been opposed by the Greek army, so the Persians hoped to land at Sounion unopposed, though they were ultimately stymied when the Greeks arrived there before them (Herodotus, *The Histories*, VI, 116). Herodotus wrote that the Persians then anchored outside of the Athenian harbor before sailing back to Asia (Herodotus, *The Histories*, VI, 116).

To add to the mystery of the shield signal, Herodotus somewhat doubted his own account. He wrote that "the tale of the Alcmaeonidae treacherously signaling to the Persians with a shield is, to me, quite extraordinary, and I cannot accept it." (Herodotus, *The Histories*, VI, 121). Herodotus' argument is that the Alcmaeonidae family helped expel the tyrants so it is difficult to believe that they would conspire with the Persians in order to re-install Hippias as tyrant. Of course, this does not necessarily mean that an Athenian traitor did not signal the Persians – it may have been a non-Alcmaeonidae or even an Alcmaeonidae with his own agenda – but at this point, the mystery of the shield signal will probably remain a permanent enigma.

As the fog from the battlefield cleared, Spartan reinforcements finally showed up, but they were no longer needed. Herodotus explained, "After the full moon, two thousand Spartans set off for Athens. They were so anxious not to be late that they were in Attica on the third day after leaving Sparta. They had, of course, missed the battle; but such was their passion to see the Persians, that they went to Marathon to have a look at the bodies. That done, they praised the Athenians on their good work, and returned home." (Herodotus, *The Histories*, VI, 120). What is most interesting about this passage is not that the Spartans showed up late for the battle - Herodotus was detailed in his explanation of their initial refusal to fight – but how quickly the

Spartans were able to make it to Marathon.

Chapter 9: How the Greeks Won the Battle of Marathon

As the Persian fleet sailed back to Ionia, the Greeks were finally able to claim victory over their foreign adversaries, but the victory was not an easy one, and there were several factors that played a role. Some of these factors were tangible and concrete, while others were more abstract, but they were all important.

The most notable factor was the battlefield strategy. Even a cursory reading of Herodotus makes it abundantly clear that Miltiades and the other Greek generals were clearly superior in their craft to Datis. Every move the Greeks made was thought out and done with consideration to what the Persian counter may be. The Greeks chose a specific route from Athens to Marathon in order to block the Persians from marching past them, then camped and advanced on terrain that made the Persian cavalry maneuvers difficult, and finally charged on foot to further mitigate what was left of any cavalry advantage. To compensate for the inferior numbers, the Greeks spread their line thin but concentrated their strongest units on the wings, where they could encircle and slaughter the Persians. On the other hand, it appears that Datis went into the battle simply thinking that his superior numbers and cavalry would be enough to carry the day. When the Greeks took his cavalry out of the equation, he apparently had no contingency plan. Even worse, he apparently didn't notice that the Greeks were concentrating their forces on the wings.

Clearly, the Greeks were one step ahead of Datis and the Persians at every stage in the battle, which may be attributed to the dictatorial style of leadership that the Persian general employed and possibly even the types of governments that the Persians and Greeks, particularly the Athenians, lived under. As Herodotus explained, the Greeks were led by a council of generals who had to come to a consensus before important strategic decisions were made. This system was an obvious benefit at the Battle of Marathon, and it was also a reflection of Athenian society, which was something that the Greeks who fought at Marathon did not want to lose. All Athenians born to Athenian citizens were conferred with citizenship rights at birth, which meant that they were able to enjoy benefits that others throughout the world, including other parts of Greece, did not have (Lloyd 1973, 42). In 490 BCE, Athens was free of her tyrants and Athenians had started to enjoy and appreciate the democratic constitution that they had instituted in their city-state. Herodotus believed that the freedom the Athenians enjoyed even made them better fighters: "For while they were oppressed under tyrants, they had no better success in war than any of their neighbors, yet, once the yoke was flung off, they proved the finest fighters in the world. This clearly shows that, so long as they were held down by authority, they deliberately shirked their duty in the field, as slaves shirk working for their masters; but when freedom was won, then every man amongst them was interested in his own cause." (Herodotus, *The Histories*, V, 78).

It is difficult to measure if the Athenians became better fighters after they instituted democracy, as Herodotus argued, but they were cognizant of the difference in political status between them and the Persians, and even their Ionian Greek cousins. Athenians were citizens who had certain rights protected by a constitution, while the Persians and even Ionians were all merely subjects of a king. It is easy to see how the Athenians would have fought much more to preserve their rights and status then the countless soldiers of the Persian army who were forced to fight.

The Athenians had much to lose in terms of their freedoms and rights, which gave them an advantage over the Persians, but defending their land was also an intangible factor that spurred the Greeks to be better fighters on the plain of Marathon. Since the Greeks were fighting in their homeland, they had the advantage of knowing how to use the terrain to their advantage, which was evidenced by the route they took to Marathon and where they camped before the battle, as well as the route they took back to Athens after the battle. Lack of knowledge of the land and terrain also played a role in the Persian retreat going awry (according to Pausanias account), as the soldiers ran into a marsh where they were then cut down.

Fighting on and for their homeland also provided the intangible benefit of fear that aroused the Greeks to fight more fiercely. After the Greeks learned the fate of Eretria, they knew that Athens would be subjected to similar destruction, which no doubt meant that every Greek fought that much harder. By 490 BCE, the Greeks also knew the fate of their Ionian cousins, who according to Herodotus were reduced to slavery. The fear of losing one's family and city can be a much more powerful incentive than any desire to capture riches that the Persian army may have had.

Pride in their status as citizens and free men definitely played a role in propelling the Greeks to victory at Marathon, but as powerful as pride can be, shame can also be strong, and it also apparently played an important role in the Greek victory at Marathon. Although Greek support for the Ionian Revolt was lukewarm at best, their withdrawal part way through the revolt was viewed by many in the Greek world as cowardly and became a source of immense shame for the Athenian people. Herodotus wrote that the Athenian shame manifested itself in a popular play that depicted the Ionian Revolt: "The Athenians, on the contrary, showed their profound distress at the capture of Miletus in a number of ways, and in particular, when Phrynichus produced his play, *The Capture of Miletus*, the audience in the theatre burst into tears. The author was fined a thousand drachmas for reminding them of their own evils, and they forbade anybody ever to put the play on stage again." (Herodotus, *The Histories*, VI, 21). The Athenian desertion of the Ionians was no doubt still fresh on the minds of the Greek warriors who took the field at Marathon as they sought to rectify a wrong that their city had done to fellow Greeks.

There were a number of intangibles that clearly contributed to Greek victory at Marathon, but perhaps the greatest Greek advantage was concrete and tangible. The standard Greek soldiers, known as hoplites, were heavily armed and well-trained fighters. Hoplites began to appear in the Hellenic world in the middle of the 8th century BCE and are named after the large shields, *hoplon*, that they used (Sage 1996, 25). Besides the shield, hoplites wore a metal (usually bronze) helmet, a bronze plate corselet, and metal greaves to protect the shins and calves (Sage 1996, 26). The primary offensive weapon of hoplites was a heavy thrusting spear that would be used when they fought in their standard *phalanx* formation, which was a type of shield wall (Sage 1996, 26). When and if the phalanx was broken, then the hoplites used short stabbing swords for close quarter combat (Sage 1996, 26). The 1st century BCE Greek historian Diodorus described how the hoplites changed weapons during a battle between the Spartans and Plataeans in the 4th century BCE: "For the most capable foot-soldiers of that time, Boeotians and Lacedaemonians, whose lines were drawn up facing one another, began the contest, exposing their lives at every risk. After the first exchange of spears in which most were shattered by the very density of the missiles, they engaged with swords." (Diodorus Siculus, *The Library of History*, XV.86, 2).

An ancient depiction of a hoplite

A 6th century BCE depiction of phalanx formations

A display of hoplite armor

The superior arms and armor of the Greek hoplites was one of the major selling points that Aristagoras argued to both the Spartans and Athenians in hopes of enticing them to join the Ionian Revolt, which he contrasted with the lack of weaponry carried by the Persian army. The Persian army was comprised of soldiers drawn from throughout the Achaemenid Empire, but at its core was a cadre of Persian fighters known as the Immortals. The Immortals were the Persian king's personal bodyguards and always numbered around 10,000, no matter the losses incurred in a battle, which is how they earned the moniker (Briant 2002, 261-63). Primary source evidence is scant concerning the armor of the Immortals, but modern scholars believe they wore a quilted corselet and carried a wicker shield (Sage 1996, 90). Remains of glazed brick reliefs from the Persian city of Susa depict the Immortals wearing long gowns with no visible armor and carrying spears with bows and quivers slung over their shoulders (Harper, Aruz, and Tallon 1992, 226-27). The Immortals may have been elite warriors, but at Marathon they were no match for the better armored Greek hoplites.

Sculpted depictions of ancient Persian warriors

A frieze from Darius I's palace believed to depict Immortals

Chapter 10: The Marathon Runner

One of the most legendary aspects of the Battle of Marathon, at least in terms of how it resonates in modern society, is the story of the runner named Phillippides or Pheidippides. According to the later Greek historian Plutarch and the 2nd century CE Greek writer Lucian, Pheidippides ran a little over 26 miles from the battlefield of Marathon to Athens in order to tell the citizens of that city that the Greeks had won the battle. Lucian wrote, "Phillippides, the one who acted as courier, is sad to have used it first in our sense when he brought the news of victory from Marathon and addressed the magistrates in session when they were anxious how the battle had ended; "Joy to you, we've won." he said, and there and then he died, breathing his last breath with that, "Joy to you." (Lucian, *A Slip of the Tongue in Greeting*, 3).

Lucian was a fiction writer and not a historian, so this account is probably more legend than historical reality, but it does reveal a couple of key aspects about the Battle of Marathon that lingered in the minds of Greeks several centuries later. First, the account shows that even those who were not historians and military officials viewed the battle as incredibly important; even if the account is purely fictional, Lucian, or whomever the fictional account began with, saw the actual battle as important enough to use as part of a literary device.

Most notably, the account has a certain resonance that has endured not only in the hearts and minds of Greeks for centuries but throughout the world. The idea of a man running to his death to give a message of victory seems to strike a chord that is difficult to describe with words, but it is eloquently done by Lucian. Of course, it is from this legend that the modern standard marathon length has been set at 26.2 miles, which is roughly the distance between Athens and the Marathon battlefield.

However, a closer examination of Herodotus' account reveals that Pheidippides probably ran a much farther distance and was nowhere near the battlefield. According to him, Pheidippides was sent by the Athenian high command to Sparta in order to elicit that city-state's support against the Persians at Marathon. He wrote, "Before they left the city, the Athenian generals sent off a message to Sparta. The messenger was an Athenian named Pheidippides, a professional long-distance runner. According to the account he gave the Athenians on his return, Pheidippides met the god Pan on Mt Parthenium, above Tegea." (Herodotus, *The Histories*, VI, 105).

As this translation of Herodotus notes, Pheidippides was one of many professional runners, who were known as *hemerodromi* in Greece and were important to interstate communication between the ancient Greek city-states (Christensen, Nielsen, and Schwartz 2009, 149). The *hemerodromi* played a vital role in ancient Greek military intelligence, as they were entrusted with classified messages that they delivered orally only to specific people (Christensen, Nielsen, and Schwartz 2009, 160). In other words, Herodotus' account of Pheidippides running to Sparta is nothing outside of the norm of standard ancient Greek military culture and therefore believable at face value. That said, Herodotus credited him with covering 500 kilometers (about 311 miles) in three days and two nights, which is much harder to take at face value (Christensen, Nielsen, and Schwartz 2009, 151).

The historicity of Pheidippides running from Athens to Sparta and back has been questioned by scholars and lay people alike for centuries, and it was apparently even the object of speculation in Herodotus' time. He noted, "The Athenians believed Pheidippides' story, and when their affairs were once more in a prosperous state, they built a shrine to Pan under the Acropolis, and from the time his message was received they have held an annual ceremony, with a torch-race and sacrifices, to court his protection. On the occasion of which I speak – when Pheidippides, that is, was sent on his mission by the Athenian commanders and said that he saw Pan – he reached Sparta the day after he left Athens and delivered his message to the Spartan government." (Herodotus, *The Histories*, VI, 105-6).

That the Athenians and Herodotus believed this story does not necessarily make it so, but modern research has revealed that the run was not only possible but even probable. In modern times, athletes have competed in numerous competitions that replicate those of the ancient Greeks, including long distance running, and in 1984, a Greek man named Giannis Kourus ran one leg of Pheidippides' journey, 250 kilometers, in under 21 hours (Christensen, Nielsen, and Schwartz 2009, 155n).

If this time was doubled, then it would be within the time that Herodotus gave, but there are other factors such as weather and diet that need to be considered. Herodotus noted that although Pheidippides successfully told the Spartans of the impending battle at Marathon, the Spartans declined on religious grounds. The account asserts, "The Spartans, though moved by the appeal, and willing to send help to Athens, were unable to send it promptly because they did not wish to break their law. It was the ninth day of the month, and they said they could not take the field until the moon was full." (Herodotus, *The Histories*, VI, 106).

Although Herodotus gave no dates concerning this event (or any having to do with the Battle of Marathon for that matter), modern scholars believe that the law in question was in relation to a festival for Apollo Karneios, which would place the date of Pheidippides' run, and the Battle of Marathon, in September 490 BCE (Christensen, Nielsen, and Schwartz 2009, 161). September in Greece is hot, which would mean that Pheidippides would have had to have consumed plenty of liquids and a high carbohydrate diet similar to other modern long distance runners in east Africa and Latin America (Christensen, Nielsen, and Schwartz 2009, 162-63). With all of these factors considered, Pheidippides would had to have averaged 10 kilometers every 48 minutes, with short breaks to eat, in order to have completed the run in the span that Herodotus mentioned (Christensen, Nielsen, and Schwartz 2009, 161).

With those factors in mind, the run would have been difficult but possible for a well-trained, professional runner. Also, as with any athletic or physical competition, a large part of the performance barriers are psychological, which Pheidippides may have overcome by meditation on the various gods, such as Pan, in order to break through the physical limitations (Lloyd 1973, 15). Fear may also have played a role in his successful run; the carnage that the Persians wrought on Eretria was no doubt still fresh on his mind as he undertook his mission to do his part to save his city. Even as the Spartans were observing their religious duties, Datis was moving the Persian army onto the plain of Marathon.

Chapter 11: The Results and Aftermath of the Battle of Marathon

After the Battle of Marathon, Darius I was not done with his punitive plans for Athens. According to Herodotus, the Persian loss at Marathon only incensed the Achaemenid king even more: "When the news of the battle of Marathon reached Darius, son of Hystaspes and king of Persia, his anger against Athens, already great enough on account of the assault on Sardis, was even greater, and he was more than ever determined to make war on Greece. Without loss of time he dispatched couriers to the various states under his dominion with orders to raise an army much larger than before; and also warships, transports, horses, and grain. So the royal command went round; and all Asia was in an uproar for three years, with the best men being enrolled in the army for the invasion of Greece, and with the preparations. In the year after that, a rebellion in Egypt, which had been conquered by Cambyses, served only to hard Darius' resolve to go to war, not only against Greece but against Egypt too." (Herodotus, *The Histories*, VII, 1).

Darius would never get his chance to exact revenge against the Athenians, as he died soon after in 487 BCE (Forrest 2001, 41), but the Greco-Persian Wars would continue with his son and successor, Xerxes, who would lead an even greater army into Greece. Some Greeks also anticipated another Persian invasion. The Spartan king Leonidas was the main advocate of this theory, sustaining it even when Darius died and was succeeded by his son Xerxes in 486 BCE. Under Leonidas and their other king, Agesilaus, the Spartans waged a series of campaigns in the years following the Battle of Marathon to bring reluctant allies and Persian sympathizers into the fold and ensure a united Greek front would greet all Persian attempts to invade.

That invasion, just as Leonidas had prophesied, came in 480 BCE, when Xerxes, at the head of an army which Herodotus claimed numbered over a million men, bridged the Hellespont (the Dardanelles straits) via a colossal pontoon bridge and marched his army into Thrace, threatening Greece proper. But ultimately, the Persian invasion under Xerxes would also end in failure thanks to legendary battles like Thermopylae and Salamis (Forrest 2001, 41), and given that perspective in hindsight, the Battle of Marathon was the pivotal event, and the Athenians were the major agent, in the Greco-Persian Wars. It was the Athenians who instigated the Ionian Greeks into rebellion and subsequently provoked the wrath of the Persians, and it was the Athenians that soundly defeated the Persians at Marathon, which set the stage for the later battles of Thermopylae, Salamis, and Plataea.

Achaemenid Persian historical records say nothing of the Battle of Marathon and little concerning the Greco-Persian wars, which is not surprising since the Persian historical tradition was essentially inherited from other ancient Near Eastern traditions that depicted the sovereign as always victorious (Cameron 1983, 80-81). Even had the Persians followed more modern or Hellenic historiographical traditions, they still would have ignored their loss at Marathon due to its one-sidedness. According to Herodotus, the final casualty count of the battle was 5,400 Persians killed while the Greeks only lost 192 men (Herodotus, *The Histories*, VI, 117).

Whatever the actual numbers, the dead Greek hoplites were buried at the site of the Battle of Marathon, which led to the site becoming both a sacred place and an archaeological treasure trove in later centuries. Modern archaeological excavations at Marathon have revealed that a mound at the site, called the "Soros," was in fact the burial place of the fallen Athenian hoplites (Hammond 1968, 14). In terms of recreating the Battle of Marathon, the mound is believed by modern scholars to be the place where the Greek center was broken and where they suffered the most casualties (Hammond 1968, 18). Excavations have shown that the hoplites were cremated *en masse* on a large pyre following ancient Greek funerary traditions. Those present for the funeral then had a large feast, placed earth over the pyre, and then laid wreaths, which effectively made the site into a memorial.

Hundreds of years later the Greek geographer Pausanias visited the site and gave a detailed report of what he witnessed. He wrote, "There is a parish called Marathon, equally distant from Athens and Carystus in Euboea. It was at this point in Attica that the foreigners landed, were defeated in battle, and lost some of their vessels as they were putting off from land. On the plain is the grave of the Athenians, and upon it are slabs giving the names of the killed according to their tribes; and there is another grave for the Boetian Plataeans and for the slaves, for slaves fought then for the first time by the side of their masters. There is also a separate monument to one man, Miltiades, the son of Cimon, although his end came later, after he had failed to take Paros and for this reason had been brought to trial by the Athenians. At Marathon every night you can hear horses neighing and men fighting. No one who has expressly set himself to behold this vision has ever got any good from it, but the spirits are not wroth with such as in ignorance change to be spectators. The Marathonians worship both those who died in the fighting, calling them heroes, and secondly Marathon, from whom the parish derives its name, and then Heracles, saying that they were the first among the Greeks to acknowledge him as a god. . . Although the Athenians assert that they buried the Persians, because in every case the divine law applies that a corpse should be laid under the earth, yet I could find no grave." (Pausanias, *Description of Greece*, I. 32. 3).

Picture of the mound at Marathon

Pausanias' account is not only interesting but also fills in gaps of Herodotus' account and corroborates it in other ways. Pausanias noted that the names of all the Athenian fallen were written on slabs at the site, which could corroborate Herodotus' number of fallen Greeks. Although Herodotus wrote his history decades after the Battle of Marathon, some of the veterans were still alive, so he may have consulted them as sources, but it is improbable that senior citizens could have given him such accurate numbers on the fallen. For that, he probably consulted the inscriptions that Pausanias described.

Another important point raised by Pausanias was that the Plataeans and slaves were given a separate grave. Herodotus made no mention of slaves fighting on the Greek side, but he did describe how the Plataeans came to side with the Athenians at Marathon. He wrote that the Plataeans were essentially compelled to fight on the side of the Athenians due to the latter's past assistance of the former and that the "people of Plataea put themselves into Athenian hands, and which led to their coming to support of Athens at Marathon." (Herodotus, *The Histories*, VI, 108). Perhaps Pausanias, who lived much later, confused the Plataeans' inferior status with some sort of servitude towards Athens, but unless more evidence is discovered, this will remain a question.

Pausanias' mention of the hero of Marathon, Miltiades, is also important, as the account notes that the general was given a memorial at Marathon but was also disgraced and faced legal problems later in his life. Herodotus gave a much more detailed account of Miltiades tragic life: "After the slaughter at Marathon, the already high reputation of Miltiades in Athens was greatly increased. Consequently, when he asked for a fleet of seventy ships together with troops and money, without even telling the Athenians the object of the expedition he had in mind, but merely saying he would enrich them if they followed him, because it was a place where they could easily get as much money as they wanted, they were so carried away by excitement that they made no objections whatever. They let him have the ships and the men, whereupon he set sail for Paros . . . All he had achieved after twenty-six days' siege was to destroy the crops in the countryside; he failed to annex the island, and he did not bring home a single penny." (Herodotus, *The Histories*, VI, 132-35).

Things only went from bad to worse for the hero of Marathon. During the siege of Paros, Miltiades suffered an injury to his leg, which became infected when he entered the sacred shrine of Demeter. On top of that, his Athenian investors pursued criminal charges against him. Herodotus wrote, "Miltiades on his return to Athens became the talk of the town; many were loud in their censure of him, and especially Xanthippus, the son of Ariphron, who brought him before the people to be tried for his life on the charge of defrauding the public. Miltiades, though present in court, was unable to speak in his own defense because his leg was gangrened; he lay on a couch and his friends spoke for him, basing their defense upon his past services to his country. They had much to say about the battle of Marathon . . . The popular verdict was to spare his life, but to fine him fifty talents for his offence. Shortly afterwards the gangrene in his thigh grew worse; mortification set in and he died. The fifty talents were paid by his son Cimon." (Herodotus, *The Histories*, VI, 136). Thus, Miltiades, the great hero of Marathon, died an early, painful, and inglorious death as a convicted criminal and pauper.

While Miltiades' life after the Battle of Marathon veered from fame to infamy, he was not the only veteran of the epic battle who was remembered in later centuries. In Pausanias's account of the Marathon battlefield, he noted that another temple was erected at the site to commemorate the Greek victory, and that a famous Greek playwright was among the veterans. He wrote, "Still farther off is a temple to Glory, this too being a thank-offering for the victory over the Persians who landed at Marathon. This is the victory of which I am of opinion the Athenians were proudest; while Aeschylus, who had won such renown for his poetry and for his share in the naval battles before Artemisium and at Salamis, recorded at the prospect of death nothing else, and merely wrote his name, his father's name, and the name of his city, and added that he had witnesses to his valor in the grove at Marathon and in the Persians who landed there." (Pausanias, *Description of Greece*, I.14.5).

Although Aeschylus was recognized as a veteran of the Battle of Marathon by ancient historians, none of his surviving works tell such stories, so it was left to other writers to glorify the Greeks. Of course, Herodotus' account is the most complete to survive, and as was the custom with ancient Greek historians, Herodotus recited his history to live audiences, which included a reading at Athens in 446/445 BCE that no doubt was in front of some of the veterans of the Battle of Marathon (Hammond 1968, 28). The Battle of Marathon also inspired the writer Lucian enough to include it in his famous *Dialogues of the Gods*, in which the god Pan discussed his attributes: "But I won't disgrace you father. I'm a musician and play the pipe loud and true. Dionysus is lost without me, and has made me his companion and fellow-reveler; I'm his dance-leader, and if you could see how many flocks I have around Tegea and on Parthenium, you'd be delighted. I'm lord and master of all Arcadia. Besides that, the other day, I fought so magnificently on the side of the Athenians at Marathon that a prize of valor was chosen for me – the cave under the Acropolis. Anyhow, go to Athens and you'll soon find out what a great name Pan has there." (Lucian, *Dialogues of the Gods*, 272).

Perhaps the greatest effect that the Battle of Marathon had on the Greek world was the level of confidence that it bestowed upon Athens. Indeed, the beginning of the 5th century BCE would usher in the Golden Age of Athens, which involved some of the city's most famous men, like Socrates and Plato. Before Marathon, Athens struggled with tyrants and numerous other Greek enemies, but after the epic battle, the Athenians went on to lead the Hellenic League, along with Sparta, successfully against the Xerxes and the Persians.

Of course, the successes would also lead Athens and Sparta on a collision course towards the Peloponnesian War in the late 5th century, a war so devastating that it would help bring about the collapse of Greek independence altogether.

Bibliography

Briant, Pierre, 2002. *From Cyrus to Alexander: A History of the Persian Empire*. Translated by Peter T. Daniels. Winona Lake, Indiana: Eisenbraums.

    Cameron, George C. "The Persian Satrapies and Related Matters." *Journal of Near Eastern Studies* 32 (1973): 47-56.

Christensen, Dirk Lund, Thomas Heine Nielsen, and Adam Schwartz. 2009. "Herodotos and *Hemerodromoi:* Pheidippides' Run from Athens to Sparta in 490 BCE from Historical and Physiological Perspectives." *Hermes* 137: 148-169.

Cameron, George C. 1983. "Ancient Persia." In *The Idea of History in the Ancient Near East*, ed. Robert C. Denton, 77-98. New Haven, Connecticut: American Oriental Society.

    ———. "The Persian Satrapies and Related Matters." *Journal of Near Eastern Studies* 32 (1973): 47-56.

Diodorus Siculus. 2004. *The Library of History*. Translated by C.H. Oldfather. Cambridge, Massachusetts: Harvard University Press.

Forrest, George. 2001. "Greece: The History of the Archaic Period." In *The Oxford History of Greece and the Hellenistic World*, edited by John Boardman, Jasper Griffin, and Oswyn Murray, 14-46. Oxford: Oxford University Press.

Hammond, N.G.L. 1968. "The Campaign and Battle of Marathon." *Journal of Hellenic Studies* 88: 13-57.

Harper, Prudence O., Joan Aruz, and Françoise Tallon, eds. 1992. *The Royal City of Susa: Ancient Near Eastern Treasures in the Louvre*. New York: Metropolitan Museum of Art.

Herodotus. 2003. *The Histories*. Translated by Aubrey de Sélincourt. London: Penguin Books.

Hodge, A. Trevor. 2001. "Reflections on the Shield at Marathon." *The Annual of the British School at Athens* 96: 237-259.

Lloyd, Alan. 1973. *Marathon: The Story of Civilizations on Collision Course*. New York: Random House.

Lucian. 1959. *Works*. Translated by K. Kilburn. Cambridge, Massachusetts: Harvard University Press.

Morkot, Robert. 1996. *The Penguin Historical Atlas of Ancient Greece*. London: Penguin Books.

Olmstead, A.T. 1948. *History of the Persian Empire.* Chicago: University of Chicago Press.

Pausanias. 1964. *Description of Greece*. Translated by W.H.S. Jones. Cambridge, Massachusetts: Harvard University Press.

Plutarch. 2005. *On Sparta*. Translated by Richard Talbert. London: Penguin Books.

———. *Lives*. 1968. Edited and translated by Bernadotte Perrin. Cambridge, Massachusetts: Harvard University Press.

Sage, Michael M. 1996. *Warfare in Ancient Greece: A Sourcebook*. London: Routledge.

Schmidt, Erich F. 1953. *Persepolis I: Structures, Reliefs, Inscriptions.* Chicago: University of Chicago Press.

Vansina, Jan. 1985. *Oral Tradition as History*. Madison: University of Wisconsin Press.

Printed in Great Britain
by Amazon.co.uk, Ltd.,
Marston Gate.